If someone were to ask me
what has been my biggest
    accomplishment in life,
I would lift my head high
and speak from my heart
    with a parent's pride
as I said the words
    "my son."

Jesse xo

Andrea Adaire Fischer

ACKNOWLEDGMENTS appear on page 48.

SPS Studios, Inc.

P.O. Box 4549, Boulder, Colorado 80306

A Son Is Forever

A Blue Mountain Arts® Collection
Featuring Poems by
Susan Polis Schutz
and Donna Fargo

Blue Mountain Press™
SPS Studios, Inc., Boulder, Colorado

Son, If I Could Have Anything in the World…

I'd wish that you would
    always be happy, forever healthy,
and that your life would be filled
    with all the things that bring you
        laughter and love.

I wish for you a life where
your dreams come true
    and your goals are achieved;
I wish that I could always
    wipe any tears from your face
and make everything okay again.

I hope you will always know
    that I am thinking about you
and forever wanting nothing more
    than your complete happiness in life.
It's your happiness that brings me
    such immense joy,
because you are my son
    and I love you so much.

— Shelly Gross

My Son, Always Remember How Proud I Am of You and How Much I Love You

You are growing up to be
an incredible young man
You are very unique and special
and I know that
your talents will give you
many paths to choose from
in the future
As you grow up, my son
always keep your many interests —
they will keep you
constantly occupied
Always keep your positive outlook —
it will give you the energy to
accomplish great things
Always keep your determination —
it will give you the ability
to succeed in meeting your goals

Always keep your excitement
about whatever you do —
it will help you to have fun
Always keep your sense of humor —
it will allow you to
make mistakes and learn from them
Always keep your confidence —
it will allow you to take risks
and not be afraid of failure
Always keep your sensitivity —
it will help you to understand
and do something about
injustices in the world
As you continue to grow
in your own unique, wonderful way
always remember that
I am more proud of you
than ever before and
I love you

—————————

Susan Polis Schutz

Son, right before my eyes, you have grown up so much on your way to becoming the special person you are today.

From a baby, to a boy, to a young man, you were full of life and filled with surprises. Trying to keep up with you has been many things: rewarding, challenging, hopeful, and fulfilling. In every one of your years, you have given me more happiness and love than most people will ever dream of.

As a family, we have walked along many paths on our way from yesterday to where we are today. Love has always been our companion, keeping us close even when we've been apart.

You have given me many gifts on that journey. But none are more precious, Son, than the smiles you give to my heart.

————————

Marin McKay

I Remember, Son…

Your years of growing,
all our shared thoughts and feelings,
the carefree and happy times
a family shares.
I remember…
the joy, the tears, and the sorrow —
stormy emotions for changing times.
I remember…
the squeeze of your hand,
whispered "I love you's,"
the snapshots and memories
of time and years.
I remember…
all the ways
you've kept my life busy.
Every day,
I celebrate and honor
all the ways
you make my heart proud.

You, Son, are loving memories,
close and strong
    and celebrated.

———————
Linda E. Knight

Someone Cares About You, and That Someone Is Me!

If you're wondering whether anyone is thinking
about you now, caring about what you're
doing, wishing you the best, and remembering
you in prayer...

If you're feeling alienated from the world, with
no one on your side, and you're questioning
if there's another human being who would
even be concerned about what's going on in
your life...

Well, wonder no more. Someone is thinking of
you and someone does care about you, and
that someone is me.

If you're wishing you had someone who hopes
that life is being good to you, that you're
coping well with every challenge and
reaching the goals you want to reach...

If you're hoping that there is someone in
    your corner of the world that you could
    call on any time, someone with whom you
    could share your hopes and dreams and
    disappointments...
Well, don't waste your time wishing and
    wondering anymore. I'd be glad to be
    that someone. All you have to do is
    let me know and I'll be there.
If you need someone to talk to, to share
    your worries with, to wish for you
    perfect health, prosperity, and peace
    and happiness...
If you want someone to point out your good
    qualities because you just need lifting up,
    someone who would be on your side no
    matter what and who would go with you
    whatever distance you have to go...
Then look no further than my direction, and
    don't give it a second thought. Know that
    someone is thinking of you and someone
    cares about you, and that someone is me.

Donna Fargo

What Is a Son?

A son is a warm spot in your heart and a smile on your lips.

In the beginning, he is charmingly innocent, putting his complete trust in you.

He comes to you for a hand to hold and for the security only your arms can provide.

He shares his tales of adventure and knows how proud you are of his discoveries and accomplishments.

All his problems can be solved by a hug and a kiss from you, and the bond you share is so strong it is almost tangible.

Times passes, and your innocent little boy starts to test his limits. He lets go of your hand to race into the midst of life without thinking ahead or looking both ways.

His problems have grown along with him, and he has learned that you can't always make his life better or kiss his troubles away.

He spends much of his time away from you, and though you long for the closeness you once shared, he chooses independence and privacy.

Discoveries and accomplishments aren't as easy to come by now, and sometimes he wonders about his worth.

But you know the worth of that young man. He is your past and your future. He is hopes and dreams that have made it through each and every disappointment and failure.

In your heart, your son is precious and treasured. Together, you struggled through the years to find the right amount of independence for each new stage of his life, until finally, you had to learn to let him go.

Now you put your trust in him, leaving that son whom you hold so dear totally in his own care. You hope he always remembers that you have a hand for him to hold and arms to provide comfort or support.

Most of all, you hope that he believes in himself as much as you believe in him, and that he knows how much you love him.

Barbara Cage

Trust in Yourself

I believe all of us have a built-in compass to help
us get to wherever we desire to go. Don't forget to
trust that compass, and refer to it often, for with that
trusting will come the strength to bear whatever life
deals you.

Don't get led astray. Ask your heart for the truth, and it
will come up with the answer and the good judgment to
make the decisions you'll need to make. Love everyone,
and don't question love's reception. Do the best you
can. Live each day as it comes. We can't get ahead of
ourselves anyway.

Remember: just as you have questions now, somewhere
inside you, and down the road, there will be better
answers and workable solutions. It takes patience and
trust to get through life's changes when you're trying
to reach goals, solve problems, and make dreams come
true. Though at times it may seem more than you can
take, I know you are strong, and you can handle
whatever comes your way. Trust in yourself.

Donna Fargo

I'll Be There for You

I will go with you through
whatever you're going through
if you want me to.

If you're down and out,
I'll be there for you.
If you're on top of the world,
I'll celebrate with you.

I'll try to ease your pain
when you're hurting;
I'll listen if you need to talk.
I'll pray for you and bear
your burdens with you.

I'll cry with you
and laugh with you.
I'll be loyal to you.

I'll wish the best for you.
I'll be there for you forever,
or for as long
as you want me.

Donna Fargo

To My Son, with Love

A mother tries to provide her son
with insight into the important
   things in life
in order to make his life
as happy and fulfilling as possible

A mother tries to teach her son
to be kind and generous towards other people
to be honest and forthright at all times
to be fair, treating men and women equally
to respect and learn from older people
to know himself well
to understand his strong and weak points
to accept criticism and learn from his mistakes
to have many interests to pursue
to have many goals to follow
to work hard to reach these goals

A mother tries to teach her son
to have a strong set of beliefs
to listen to his intelligence
to laugh and enjoy life
to appreciate the beauty of nature
to express his feelings openly
   and honestly at all times
that he does not always have to be strong and stoic
that he should not be afraid to show his emotions
to realize that love is the best emotion
   that anyone can have
to value the family unit as the basis of all stability

If I have provided you with an insight
into most of these things
then I have succeeded as a mother
in what I hoped to accomplish in raising you
If many of these things slipped by
while we were all so busy
I have a feeling that you know them anyway
And as your proud mother
I will always continue to love and support
everything you are and everything you do
I am always here for you, my son
I love you
_____
Susan Polis Schutz

Son, I've Always Had So Many Wishes for You

When you were so small, I wished
　　you could talk.
As you struggled to crawl, I wished
　　you could walk.
When your room was so messy,
　　I wished it was neat.
While you played with your food,
　　I wished you would eat.
When you learned how to drive,
　　I wished you would wait.
I wished you home safely,
　　not out on a date.
And now, as I've watched you
　　become a young man,
setting out on your own to learn
　　all that you can
from books and from life,
　　I want you to know
I stand proudly behind you,
　　wherever you go.
I have dreams for you and one wish,
　　just one:
I wish we had more time together,
　　my son.

Diane Sieverson

Twelve Tips to Help You Through Life

1. <u>Shine</u>… with your God-given talents.
2. <u>Sparkle</u>… with interest when you
   listen to others.
3. <u>Twinkle</u>… with a sense of humor,
   and you'll never take life
   too seriously.
4. <u>Sing</u>… to keep up your spirits.
5. <u>Pray</u>… and you'll know you're
   never alone.
6. <u>Unwrap</u>… your dreams and make
   them happen.
7. <u>Celebrate</u>… your every step to success.
8. <u>Decorate</u>… your own space and make
   it your peaceful retreat.
9. <u>Play</u>… with passion after you
   work hard.
10. <u>Exchange</u>… your doubts for hopes;
    your frowns for smiles.
11. <u>Make</u>… cookies, friends, happiness.
12. <u>Believe</u>… in the spirit of life
    and in your power to make the
    world a better place.

———————————
Jacqueline Schiff

My Son, I Will Always
Do My Best for You

Sometimes it is so hard
to be a parent
We never know for sure
if what we are doing or
how we are acting is right

Sometimes it might seem
like I make a decision
that is not fair
I might not be
looking at the immediate results
but I am thinking
how it will affect you
and what you will learn from it
    in the future

Since I consider you
a very smart person
capable of leading your own life
I very rarely
make decisions for you
But when I do
I want you to know that
I have a great amount of
sensitivity to who you are and
the foundation of any suggestions
I give to you
are made with
an enormous love and respect
for you
my son
—————————
Susan Polis Schutz

If There's a Dream
in Your Heart...
Go for It!

If you're treading new ground
or fighting the same old battle,
   don't give up.
Continue to dream, plan, and do.
Try something different if you're stuck.
Do whatever your heart tells you.
Give yourself credit for all you've
   accomplished.
Most dreams that come true are born
   out of desire
and fueled by preparation and action.
Don't be afraid. You can do it.
I know you can.

———————
Donna Fargo

My Son, You Have
What It Takes to Be a Success

It takes a lot to set your
sights on a distant horizon
and keep on reaching for
your goals. It takes a lot...
of courage and hard work,
believing and achieving,
patience and perseverance,
inner strength and gentle
hope. It takes a lot of giving
it your best and doing the
fantastic things you do.

But most of all...

It takes someone as
wonderful as
you.

— Alin Austin

Son, I Want to Share
These Thoughts with You

No matter where you go in this world,
here are a few things
I hope you'll remember...

Always hold honor as a high virtue.
    Despite how the world may be,
    rise above.
Always speak the truth, because others
    will hold you in high esteem as a
    man who can be trusted.
Never lose faith in your fellow human
    beings, despite times when they
    may let you down. Never forget
    to thank God for the opportunities
    you've been given.

Believe in hard work. No one will hand
   you the future you want. The ladder
   to success is steep, but take one step
   at a time and you'll get to the top.
No matter where you go or what
   mistakes you make, remember that
   your family will always be here for
   you. That's how deep love goes.
Always believe in yourself. Your
   happiness depends on no one else
   but you. If there is something that
   you are unhappy about, you must
   change it.
Always hold love close to you. When
   you make a commitment, cherish it
   for the rest of your life.

Sherrie L. Householder

You've Got a Family Who Loves You, and You're Always Welcome Home

When words from the heart fail to make
    the desired connection,
When you're just tired of eating out and trying
    to please other people in your life,
When you need to know there's someone who
    really cares about what you're going
    through and how you're feeling,
We all need a sense of belonging sometimes.
That's the time to remember...
    You've got a family who loves you,
        and you're always welcome home.

Whether you need some understanding, an
    extra blanket for your bed, the arms of
    loved ones to hold you, a favorite dessert
    to make you feel special,
If you want someone to talk to, to listen to,
    to cry with, or just be with...
We are here and we'll never turn our backs on
    you, no matter what you're going through.

You don't have to share everything with us
    if you don't want to,
But we just want you to remember...
    You've got a family who loves you,
        and you're always welcome home.

We're here to talk about your needs, your
    hopes and plans, your disappointments,
    whatever is in your heart and on your mind.
We're not perfect, but we're here for you,
    not to judge you, but to accept you,
    to love you without condition,
    to be with you wherever you are.
So, no matter what you're going through,
    no matter what we need to do for you,
Always remember...
    You've got a family who loves you,
        and you're always welcome home.

———————————

Donna Fargo

Know What It Means
to Be a Man, My Son...

A man is someone who realizes
   that strength of character
is more important than being tough.
He can be tender and kind,
   and he doesn't misuse his authority.
He is generous, and enjoys
   giving as well as receiving.
A man is understanding;
   he tries to see both sides
      of a situation.
He is responsible;
   he knows what needs to be done,
      and he does it.
He is trustworthy;
   his word is his honor.
He loves humor, and looks
   at the bright side of things.
He takes time to think
   before he reacts.
He loves life, nature, discovery,
   excitement, and so much more.
He is a little boy sometimes,
   living in an adult body
and enjoying the best of both worlds.

———————
Barbara Cage

...But Don't Ever Let Go
of That Little Boy Inside

Within the soul of every man
lives the little boy he once was —
a boy who looked at the world
    through eyes of wonder
and always hungered for new sights
    and far-off horizons;
who woke up each morning
    bursting with energy
and anticipation for the day ahead;
who believed in "once upon a time..."
and planned to conquer the world
    before dinner.
Don't ever let go of this little boy.
Let his spirit reawaken you
to all the potential that exists
    in your life.
Remember how it felt to believe
    you could be or do anything
        you imagined,
and bring some of that same power
    to your life today.
Honor the little boy within you...
and he will help you to become
    the great man you're meant to be.

Edmund O'Neill

Son

If you could have only one memory of us, I hope we have shown you how very much we love you.

It isn't always easy being a parent. We didn't know exactly what we were doing at times, even though we might have acted as though we did. Our intentions were always good, but as you know by now, much of life is a trial, with few guarantees. We tried to provide you with the best foundation we could and to instill in you the confidence and assurance that you can handle whatever comes your way. We tried to pass on to you a healthy emotional-support system, a strong spiritual base, and good moral values. When you went off in search of your own destiny, we hoped you would feel thankful, secure, prepared, and, most of all, loved.

There were times when we were too easy on you and times when we weren't easy enough. By fostering your interests and nurturing your strengths, we wanted to give you not only enough freedom to develop into your own uniqueness, but also enough discipline to make your own choices and help you deal with the challenges you would inevitably face.

I'm sure there were times when we missed the mark, but we hope that your memories are positive and whatever impressions we've made on you are life-enhancing.

We hope you're enjoying life and growing in wisdom every day. We hope you're happy with yourself and the choices you've made. We trust that you will handle whatever challenges you face with grace and ease. We pray for your safety, good health, prosperity, and happiness. Because of your attitude, common sense, and good judgment, we know you will grow in patience and understanding as you turn every obstacle into just another challenge to teach you and guide you on the path to victory and a happy life.

We want you to know that we're proud of you. We think you're wonderful, and we feel so lucky to be your parents. We hope you know that we couldn't ask for a better son, and we love you very much.

———————

Donna Fargo

My Son, I Hope that All Your Dreams Become a Reality, and I Love You

Dreams can come true if you take the time to
think about what you want in life...
Get to know yourself
Find out who you are
Choose your goals carefully
Be honest with yourself
But don't think about yourself so much
that you analyze every word and action
Don't become preoccupied with yourself
Find many interests and pursue them
Find out what is important to you
Find out what you are good at
Don't be afraid to make mistakes
Work hard to achieve successes
When things are not going right
don't give up — just try harder
Find courage inside of you to remain strong
Give yourself freedom to try out new things

Don't be so set in your ways that you can't grow
Always act in an ethical way
Laugh and have a good time
Form relationships with people you respect
Treat others as you want them to treat you
Be honest with people
Accept the truth
Speak the truth
Open yourself up to love
Don't be afraid to love
Remain close to your family
Take part in the beauty of nature
Be appreciative of all that you have
Help those less fortunate than you
Try to make other lives happy
Work towards peace in the world
Live life to the fullest
My son, dreams can come true
and I hope that all your dreams become a reality
I love you

Susan Polis Schutz

Be the Best
that You Can Be

Everyone has special qualities and attributes to offer that no one else has. Be thankful for yours and the grace by which you've received them. Accept them with humility and share them. Don't be afraid to be yourself; don't be afraid you're not good enough.

Always commit yourself to excellence and be the best that you can be, for your own integrity. The more you practice your talent and cultivate your specialty, the happier you will be and the more creative you'll become in applying yourself.

You know yourself better than anyone, so set your own limits. Think your own thoughts. Dream your own dreams. Make your own plans. Do your own thing. Make your actions line up with what you really believe.

Be yourself; you're no better or worse than anyone else. Be the best that you can be and accept that as enough.

Donna Fargo

You Can Do Anything
You Believe You Can

If there's a goal you want to reach, resolve to start
doing something about it. Stop procrastinating.
Write out what you want to do and how you plan
to do it. It's the same as if you were planning a trip:
you get a map, make your preparations, and then
start traveling the right road.

Do something every day to move the roadblocks that
stand in your way. Keep it simple. Trust your instincts.
Do one thing at a time. Remember... if you haven't
reached your goal and you keep doing the same
things you're doing now, you will keep ending up
in similar places to where you are now.

Once you start making progress, you will be magically
propelled toward eventual reward. Just keep listening
and taking direction from inside you. Every effort
you make tells your being that you're serious. Action
empowers us toward more action. Be patient; your
dreams will not come true overnight. But start now,
and go with love and courage and confidence. Don't
be afraid. You can do anything you believe you can.

Donna Fargo

In Admiration
of You, My Son

If someone were to ask me
what has been my biggest
   accomplishment in life,
I would lift my head high
and speak from my heart
   with a parent's pride
as I said the words
   "my son."
I would speak about the good fortune
   and blessing of having a son
who spreads happiness and comfort
to all who cross his path;
a son who puts the concerns of others
   ahead of his own;
a son who has grown from
   an enchanting young boy
into a compassionate, courageous man;
a son who has grown up knowing
the value of respect
and who has earned the admiration
   of those who know him.

You have so many wonderful qualities
that my words to describe them
    would be endless —
much like my pride in you.
You have given so much joy
    to my life,
and I am overcome with feelings
    of tranquillity
whenever I think about who and what
    you've become.
You are my biggest and greatest
    accomplishment.
You have given my life more meaning
    and happiness
than you could ever know.
I love you.

Andrea Adaire Fischer

You're the Best
Son in the World!

I couldn't ask for a better son. You listen. You show your appreciation. You are honorable. You have a giving heart and a loving spirit. I believe these are the best gifts we can possess to nurture our lives and help us to be of service to others.

You search your heart and try to practice the golden rule. You treat others with respect and gentleness. You seem to know instinctively that to do good things in the world, we must start with ourselves, making the grade one thought and one behavior and one action at a time. You're slow to anger, slow to judge, and quick to forgive.

You don't go along with the crowd just because it's popular, and you give others the benefit of the doubt. These are valuable qualities, and I realize I may be prejudiced, but I am proud to see these virtues in you and pleased to call you my son.

So, keep on doing what you're doing and being who you are. I'm so proud of you, Son, and I would sing your praises to anyone. I just wanted you to know how thankful I am for you. It gives me great pleasure to have you as my son.

———————
Donna Fargo

Poems to Help My Son Be Strong Along the Path of Life

"Always keep your goodness
and never lose your love.
For then, Son, you'll be
rewarded with success
in ways you never dreamed of."

"You can be head and shoulders above the crowd.
You don't have to be a giant to be strong.
Walk tall and be proud. All you have to be...
is someone people look up to."

"In the course of time, you will be reminded
that hard work gets good results and keeping
healthy is essential. Know when to work your mind
and let your body relax, and know when doing just
the opposite makes the most sense. Being able
to handle whatever life brings your way
is not a matter of coincidence."

"You've already got a good idea of what is expected of you and wished for you. One of the best things you can accomplish on life's pathway is to be a walking example of the golden rule. Don't let anyone fool you into thinking that it is worthless; it is one of the most valuable things you can do."

"You've got so many possibilities ahead! Don't be too quick to limit your choices of what to do, because you might limit your chances of unimagined joys that are waiting just for you."

"You've got a wonderful sense of humor and a good outlook on life. Let those qualities help to see you through when you're deciding where to go and you're not sure what to do."

"You've got a big heart. Keep it filled with happiness. You've got a fascinating mind. Keep finding new ways to grow. Keep yearning. Keep learning. Keep trying. Keep smiling. And keep remembering that a parent's love goes with you... everywhere you go."

Douglas Richards

Son, Remember This...

I'll always love you. Remember... as you read these words, that I'll hold you in a very precious place in my heart — not just today, but as long as there are stars in the sky.

Remember that — if I could — I would give you the moon and the sun in return for all the smiles and memories you've given me.

And remember that when I say "I love you," I want you to know what those words really mean. "I love you" means that you're the most wonderful son there could ever be. It means that you have made me more proud of you than you could even begin to imagine. And it means that I will never let a day go by without feeling blessed by the giving... of a gift like you.

Laurel Atherton

To My Son, with Love

From the day you
were born
you were
so special
so smart
so sensitive
so good
It was fun
to be with you

As you grew
you became your
own person
with your own ideas
with your own way
of doing things
It was exciting
to watch you

As you grew more
you became independent
still special
still smart
still sensitive
still good
I am so proud
of the person you are
and I want you to always know
that I devotedly love you

Susan Polis Schutz

My Son, Never Forget
How Much I Love You

When you were very, very small,
I used to dance with you
    cradled in my arms.
You were my precious angel,
and when I held you close,
love overwhelmed me.

I used to wonder what kind of life
    you would lead.
What would be your first word,
    your first job?
What kind of man would you become?
And would your life take you
    far away from me?

Then I'd hold you even closer.
I'd give you an extra kiss
and an extra squeeze,
and whisper "I love you" one more time.
I knew you were too young to remember
    my words,
but I prayed you would never forget them.

Now you are a man.
There are days when I still long
    to cradle you in my arms
and dance with you once again.
Although I miss my little boy,
I am so proud of the man you are
and of who you will become.
When I think of you,
love still overwhelms me.
And as we both grow older
and memories fade,
please never forget these words
that you were once too small
    to remember:
"I love you." *Jesse* ✗ O

Kathryn Higginbottom Gorin

You're Everything a Son Should Be

Throughout your life,
I have seen how each and every step
   that you took
led you away from me
   and toward your independence.
Yet often, you didn't even notice
   that it was occurring.

The memories I have of you
   still stir in my heart.
Sometimes, they cause me to
   stop what I'm doing
and regret the quick passage of time.
I'm amazed that my little boy
   now looks out at me from
     a grown man's body.

As you move on to new adventures,
I'll be there to support you
   and believe in you.
I am so proud of all that
   you've accomplished;
you've become the type of man
   I always hoped you would be.
(I just wish it hadn't happened so fast!)

—————
Barbara Cage

To My Son, I Love You

I feel so fortunate to have you for a son
I love your bright face
when we talk seriously about the world
I love your smile
when you laugh at the inconsistencies in the world
I love your eyes
when you are showing emotion
I love your mind
when you are discovering new ideas
and creating dreams to follow
Many people tell me that
they cannot talk to their children
that they cannot wait for them to leave home
I want you to know
that I enjoy you so much and
I look forward to any time we can spend together
Not only are you my adored son
but you are also my friend
I am so proud of you
my son and
I love you

Susan Polis Schutz

ACKNOWLEDGMENTS

The following is a partial list of authors whom the publisher especially wishes to thank for permission to reprint their works.

Diane Sieverson for "Son, I've Always Had So Many Wishes for You." Copyright © 2001 by Diane Sieverson. All rights reserved.

The following works have previously appeared in Blue Mountain Arts® publications:

"What Is a Son?" by Barbara Cage, "Poems to Help My Son Be Strong Along the Path of Life" by Douglas Richards, "Son, I Want to Share These Thoughts with You" by Sherrie L. Householder, "Son, If I Could Have Anything in the World..." by Shelly Gross, "Son, right before my eyes..." by Marin McKay, "You're Everything a Son Should Be" and "A man is someone who..." by Barbara Cage, "My Son, You Have What It Takes to Be a Success" by Alin Austin, "Twelve Tips to Help You Through Life" by Jacqueline Schiff, "In Admiration of You, My Son" by Andrea Adaire Fischer, "My Son, Never Forget How Much I Love You" by Kathryn Higginbottom Gorin, "I Remember, Son..." by Linda E. Knight, "Within the soul of every man..." by Edmund O'Neill, and "Son, Remember This..." by Laurel Atherton. Copyright © 1996, 1997, 1998, 1999, 2000, 2001 by SPS Studios, Inc. All rights reserved.

SPS STUDIOS, INC., P.O. Box 4549, Boulder, Colorado 80306.